CW00549268

From Letterkenny, County Donegal, John D. Ruddy is a writer, actor, teacher, illustrator and historian. He is the creator of Manny Man and the YouTube history series Manny Man Does History, including World War I in 6 Minutes, Irish History in 6 Minutes and Easter Rising in 8 Minutes. When not writing and illustrating history videos, John is usually treading the boards of the Irish stage as a professional actor, or in the classroom talking about history.

Stay up to date with the author at:

 www.twitter.com/JohnDRuddy

 www.facebook.com/JohnDRuddy

 www.youtube.com/c/JohnDRuddyMannyMan

In memory of
Kathleen Ruddy,
bringing me rainbows
wherever I go!

MANNY MAN DOES THE HISTORY OF IRELAND

BY JOHN D. RUDDY

The Collins Press

FOREWORD

This book goes out to all the boring history teachers I've ever had.

    History is important! There, I said it. It plays such a vital role in our lives whether we like it or not. It hangs like a shadow over the decisions we make and it acts as a reminder of what could go wrong but also what could go right.

    History can so easily be destroyed by lists of dates and names. I try to find the story within history. The cause and effect. The chain reaction. The ripples turning into waves as they push out from an event into the future.

    A deeper understanding of history allows us to see where we have come from but also where we may be going to. As Winston Churchill once said, 'The farther back you look, the farther forward you are likely to see.' I wonder if he saw how the Ireland situation would unfold.

20,000 BCE The Ice Age

IRELAND

Europe towards the end of the last Ice Age. Notice some land bridges that don't exist today!

The beginning of people in Ireland goes back to the end of the Ice Age. The huge glaciers and ice sheets that once covered most of Europe began to thaw. As the land became more hospitable animals moved in, and early humans followed them to hunt!

8000 BCE

The first people in Ireland were hunter-gatherers, which does exactly what it says on the tin: they hunted animals and gathered fruit and berries for survival. They lived in small social groups and had a great knowledge of how to live off the land, when to hunt and when to gather.

The Great Irish Deer was a huge deer that lived in Western Europe towards the end of the Ice Age. Ireland was one of the last places they were found before they went extinct. They are often referred to as the Great Irish Elk, which is a mistake! They were deer, not elk (a moose).

3200 BCE The Stone Age

Eventually farming came to Ireland, growing crops and animals so you didn't have to go and hunt/gather them! Early farmers began clearing forest for farmland. The forests had stopped too much rain from getting into the soil, but once they were cleared, the rain saturated the farmland, turning it into bog, not what the farmers had wanted. Old Stone Age walls can still be found today under the bog in the Céide Fields, County Mayo. One thing people were really good at was making tools. Nothing went to waste! They made clothes from animal skin and tools from bones, wood and stone.

Stone Age community

SHE BE A FINE FIELD!!

MOOO!

An early stone Age farmer

Stone Age axe

8

Newgrange under construction

Stone Age people had a great awareness of the sun and how it moved. They probably believed it was a god that brought the light and warmth during the daytime, making the crops grow. As the year went on, the sun would get lower and lower as the winter came and the land began to die. People back then might not have trusted that the sun would

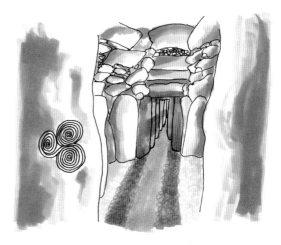

The sun entering the chamber of Newgrange on the Winter Solstice (21 December)

return! They built many passage tombs and stone circles to mark the movement of the sun throughout the year. The most famous tomb today is Newgrange, which is older than Stonehenge or the Pyramids of Giza. Newgrange and many other Megalithic ('big stone') tombs line up with the sun on special days in the year: the solstices and equinoxes. Thankfully the sun kept coming back!

Newgrange today

500 BCE The Celts

Celtic culture spread out from central Europe and reached those islands of what would become Britain and Ireland. The Celts brought with them their languages, art, pottery and their ability to make tools from the metal bronze.

Some Celtic languages still survive today, such as Irish (of course) in Ireland, Scots Gaelic in Scotland, Manx on the Isle of Man, Cornish in Cornwall and Breton in Brittany, France.

WHO DID YOU CALL GINGER!?!

The Celts were fierce warriors and sometimes went into battle with no armour, to intimidate their enemies! Spears and short swords were their weapons of choice.

Celtic sun god Lugh

100 BCE

The Celts loved their music and art...
and fighting with each other a lot...
and stealing cows... a lot. Cows were like
currency to the Celtic people and cattle
raids were a common way for one clan
to get one over on another clan.

TÁ AN CRAIC MIGHTY!

Cattle raids were a big thing in Celtic Ireland,
so much so that they inspired a great legend,
the Táin Bó Cúailnge (Cattle Raid of Cooley).

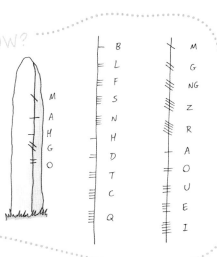

DID YOU KNOW?

Ogham was a very old form of
writing used by the people of Ireland.
It used straight lines and was usually
carved into the corners of special tall
stones, called ogham stones. It was
read from bottom to top.

500 BCE Celtic Mythology

By the time the Celtic culture came to Ireland, people had forgotten who built the tombs and explained them with awesome stories of giants, heroes and faeries. The storytelling tradition in Ireland was very strong and the travelling storyteller was a very important person in society!

Balor of the Evil Eye

Portal Dolmens were burial structures built by Stone Age people. Celtic people believed them to be a portal to the land of the faeries.

DID YOU KNOW?

Cúchulainn

Such great characters from Celtic Mythology included Balor of the Evil Eye, who was a giant with a powerful, poisonous eye who lived on Tory Island, and Cúchulainn, who was a legendary warrior. When he was a young fella he was known as Setanta and was a skilled athlete. He was invited to a feast held by a smith named Culann. Setanta was running late and Culann had already set his hound to guard the area.

The hound spotted latecomer Setanta and bounded for him but Setanta whacked his sliotar at the hound, killing him. Culann was impressed with this, despite losing his hound and hired Setanta as a replacement. And so he became Cúchulainn, the Hound of

Culann. In later life, Cúchulainn fought off the armies of Queen Maeve until he died of exhaustion, strapped to a rock.

The Morrigan was the Celtic goddess of war and often took the form of a raven. Ravens and crows would often be seen flying over the battlefield waiting for a free meal afterwards!

The Celts also invented Halloween, when they sacrificed animals and possibly even people in great bonfires to keep the faeries away from their door and welcome the dead back for one night. It was Oíche Shamhna, the Night of Samhain, the death of summer, and it marked the beginning of the winter. People hoped they would survive until spring!

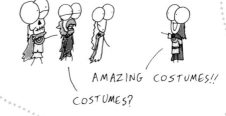

AMAZING COSTUMES!!

COSTUMES?

432 CE Early Christianity

Christianity, the belief in Jesus Christ, had spread across Europe partly due to the Roman Empire but it hadn't yet taken off in Ireland. A young boy named Patricius (Patrick) from Wales was captured by Irish raiders and brought back as a slave to Ireland. While there he discovered that the Irish didn't believe in Jesus. He managed to escape his slavery but wanted to return and teach people about Christianity. In around 432 St Patrick returned and brought Christianity to Ireland, challenging the druids who were the powerful priests within the Celtic culture. Legend has it that he used the shamrock to explain the Holy Trinity, three leaves but one leaf. It is also said that St Patrick banished the snakes from Ireland but there weren't any snakes in Ireland to begin with! It may refer to the druids and how the snake in Christianity was seen as the devil.

I'M NOT SURE IF I WORE A LOT OF GREEN... OR BANISHED SNAKES... OR USED SHAMROCKS...

St Patrick died on 17 March and it is remembered today as St Patrick's Day, which has become a huge day worldwide, celebrating Irish culture.

532

The early Christians in Ireland very wisely incorporated old Celtic traditions into Christianity, resulting in things like the old spring goddess Brigid becoming St Brigit, not to mention St Patrick making a cameo appearance at the end of the much older story of the Children of Lir in which four children are cursed and turned into swans by their wicked stepmother.

The St Brigit's Cross is probably a tradition that was in Ireland long before Christianity, but it became associated with St Brigit.

St Brigit's Day is on 1 February and on the night before, the cross is made from rushes and left out that night in a white cloth to be blessed. It marks the beginning of spring and lines up with the older Celtic festival of Imbolc.

521-597 Monks and Monasteries

St Colmcille

St Colmcille

As Christianity became the main religion of Ireland, monks began building monasteries in which they would live, work and pray. One notable monk was St Colmcille (St Columba) who was a very powerful man and set up many monasteries. He was born in Gartan in the north-west of Ireland. His name, Colmcille, means 'Dove of the Church'.

560-561

Colmcille was even involved in history's first copyright dispute! Colmcille had copied St Finnian's manuscript and planned to keep the copy for himself.

LIKE MY WORK?

St Colmcille

THAT'S MY WORK!!

St Finnian

St Finnian claimed ownership of the copy too, as it was based on his work. They brought the dispute to the king who said 'to every cow its calf, to every book its copy'.

Colmcille's supporters didn't like this. They went to war and fought at the Battle of Cúl Dreimhne (The Battle of the Book) but they lost. Having been the cause of so much death and destruction, Colmcille banished himself from Ireland and set up a

THE BATTLE OF THE BOOK

monastery on the island of Iona off the coast of Scotland from which he would send out missionaries to build monasteries across England such as Lindisfarne. Many historians reckon it was on Iona that work began on what became the Book of Kells, possibly by St Colmcille himself!

SO LONG, IRELAND! I'LL NEVER LOOK BACK... MAYBE ONCE...

Colmcille would return only once to Ireland after his banishment, when he was summoned to a political high council of chieftains and important people. Because he had vowed never to set foot on Irish soil or lay eyes on Ireland again, he returned blindfolded with sods of Scottish Iona soil strapped to his feet!

OK, I'M BACK!

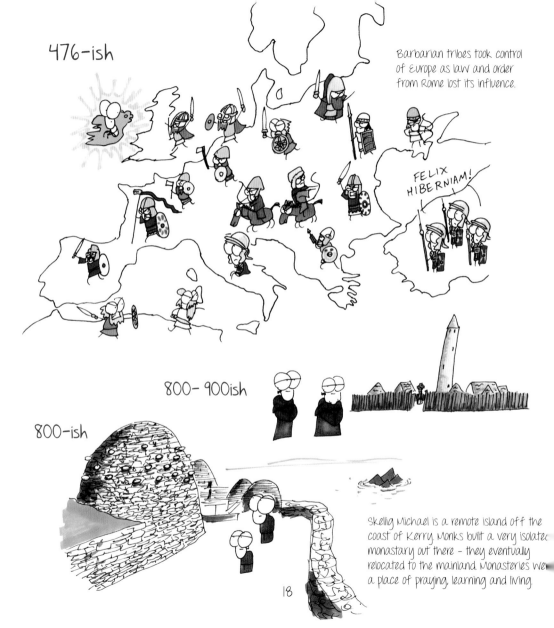

476-ish

Barbarian tribes took control of Europe as law and order from Rome lost its influence.

FELIX HIBERNIAM!

800-900ish

800-ish

Skellig Michael is a remote island off the coast of Kerry. Monks built a very isolated monastary out there - they eventually relocated to the mainland. Monasteries were a place of praying, learning and living.

18

While the rest of Europe fell apart after the end of the Roman Empire, Ireland enjoyed probably one of the most productive times in its history as the monks in their monasteries produced beautiful treasures and books. Many scholars travelled to Ireland for the peace and quiet to study. This is when Ireland became known as the Isle of Saints and Scholars.

The Book of Kells is a beautifully decorated manuscript containing the four gospels. It was (probably) started on Iona under St Colmcille and was completed by several different monks over many, many years. The artwork is amazingly intricate and the shiny inks layered onto the vellum (calfskin) pages almost make it come to life on the page! It can be found in the Old Library of Trinity College Dublin today.

High crosses had Bible scenes carved onto them and were used to teach the largely illiterate population the stories of the Bible. Most of them would probably have been painted colourfully when they were originally made. Muiredach's Cross (left) can be found in Monasterboice, County Louth.

The Ardagh Chalice is one of many fine examples of the wonderfully detailed metalwork produced in medieval Ireland. It would've been used to hold Holy Communion in the monasteries. Its shape and design was the basis for the Sam Maguire Cup for the Gaelic Athletic Association. The Ardagh Chalice can be found in the National Museum, Dublin.

795 Vikings in Ireland

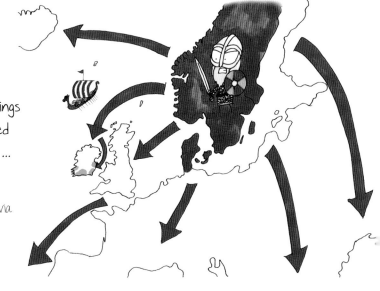

B ut then the Vikings came and ruined everything!! Sort of ...

The Viking home of Scandinavia is marked in red on the map.

Viking longships had fierce beasts carved into them to look scary!

The Vikings were from Scandinavia (Norway, Sweden and Denmark). Scandinavia was tough, with very harsh winters. The men from these places travelled all over Europe in their longships, raiding and trading. Some Vikings even went as far as North America in their adventures (long before Christopher Columbus!).

Vikings raiding an Irish monastery.

VIKINGS DIDN'T AVE HORNED HELMETS!!!

A Viking warrior equipped with spear, axe, long sword, helmet, shield, tunic and chainmail.

The Vikings were fierce warriors who used tough iron weapons and armour. Their swords were long and effective! When they came to Ireland, they raided the monasteries and stole their treasures. The Vikings were not Christians at first and believed in the Norse gods, such as Thor, Freya, Loki and Odin, and despite the common image, Vikings did not have horns on their helmets! Try raising an axe above your head with a horned helmet – most impractical!

HMM... THIS PLACE IS A LITTLE LESS COLD, A LITTLE MORE WET. LET'S STAY!

I THOUGHT THE MEDITERRANEAN WOULD'VE BEEN NICER!

But apparently they liked Ireland so much that some of them decided to stay. They set up Dublin along with most of the major ports on the island. Whereas most Irish place names we have today are derived from the Irish language, some place names are from the old Viking names, such as Wicklow (Vikinga-ló: 'Meadow of the Vikings'), Wexford (Veisafjǫrðr: 'Fjord of the Mud Flats') and Waterford (Veðrafjǫrðr: 'Ram Fjord').

VIKING IRELAND

LIMERICK

CORK

DUBLIN

WICKLOW

WEXFORD

WATERFORD

Map of the major Viking ports in Ireland

The Viking settlement at Dublin began around 841 and slowly grew as a successful port. Where the River Poddle flowed into the wide River Liffey, the Vikings built thatched houses and fortifications. The main fortification, which would become the castle, was built alongside the River Poddle, which acted as a natural moat. On this corner, the Poddle gathered into a large black pool or 'Dubh Linn' in Irish which is where Dublin gets its name!

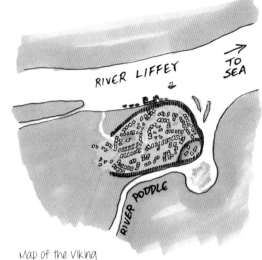

Map of the Viking settlement of Dubh Linn

DUBLINIA

23

1014 The Battle of Clontarf

As the Vikings grew in power in Dublin, the High King of Ireland, Brian Ború, led an army against the Vikings. On 23 April 1014, a huge battle was fought not far from Dubh Linn at Clontarf, north of the mouth of the River Liffey.

Brian Ború

A map showing the various kingdoms and territories in Ireland in 1014

Brian Ború's forces fought a Viking-Irish alliance in a battle that lasted the whole day. Thousands of men were killed and even though Brian's forces won, Brian himself was killed by the Viking leader Brodir while Brian prayed in his tent. After the defeat, the Vikings were no longer as powerful in Ireland.

1066 The Norman Invasion

The Normans were powerful, armour-clad men who came from Normandy (hence their name), in the north of what is now France. The Normans conquered the Anglo-Saxons of England in 1066 at the Battle of Hastings and very quickly their rule and culture took over in England.

The Normans were descended from settled Norsemen from Northern Europe. They were very good at making effective iron armour and weapons, which made them very tough to kill. Their swords had a new feature, the cross-guard, which would stop an enemy blade hurting your hand (hopefully). It was the height of weapons technology at the time! They were also skilled horsemen.

NORMANDY

NO, MY NAME ISN'T **NORMAN**... I GET ASKED THAT A LOT!

1167

About a hundred years after conquering England, the Normans came to Ireland, having been invited by the King of Leinster to help win his throne. Diarmaid Mac Murchada was the King of Leinster but wanted to become the High King of Ireland. He sought help from his neighbours in England. He raised a force led by Richard de Clare, aka Strongbow. Mac Murchada promised his daughter Aoife as a wife to Strongbow. Strongbow came to Ireland, defeated the Vikings and the Irish and handed control of Dublin, Waterford and many fortresses to the English King Henry II. Strongbow married Aoife and Strongbow ultimately became King of Leinster.

Richard de Clare, aka 'Strongbow'

Thus began what became the Norman rule, which spread across Ireland.

1170

HERE, STRONGBOW! HAVE MY DAUGHTER!

AW, THANKS!

1224 Norman Ireland

The Normans built the first castles in Ireland and set up more towns. The Gaelic Irish lived in much more rural and agricultural communities. Over the centuries, the Gaelic chieftains had built stone forts for defence. Crannógs were also defensive dwellings built out of wood by the Gaelic Irish, on islands. The Normans built whole defensive complexes with stone: huge castles with defensive walls, e.g. Trim Castle, County Meath. Sometimes entire towns were surrounded by walls, e.g. Athenry, County Galway. The area around Dublin was known as The Pale and was under the control of the English King. As the Normans settled in Ireland they integrated into a lot of Irish culture initially, particularly beyond The Pale.

A Norman castle vs a Gaelic crannóg

CASTLE ENVY?

SHUT UP!

1348

Because the Gaelic Irish didn't live in towns much, when the Black Death reached Ireland, the Normans were much more affected. The Black Death was the spread of the bubonic plague across Europe. It killed an estimated 30-60% of Europe's population. It was spread by the fleas on the backs of rats. It spread widely from place to place on merchant ships.

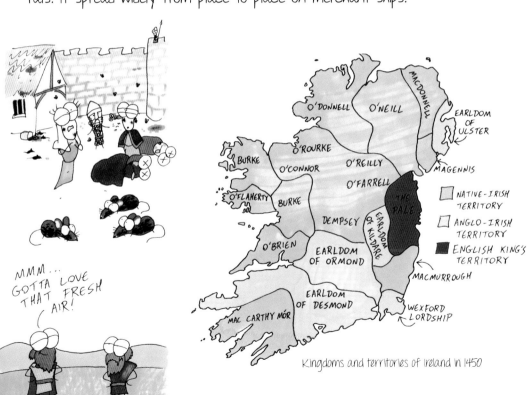

MMM...
GOTTA LOVE
THAT FRESH
AIR!

Kingdoms and territories of Ireland in 1450

1366 The Statutes of Kilkenny

Over the years, the Normans living in Ireland really bought into Irish culture, speaking the Irish language and marrying into Irish families. The English were worried that the Normans in Ireland were becoming more Irish than the Irish and so they banned them from marrying into Irish families or speaking the Irish language in the very strict new laws, the Statutes of Kilkenny.

Coat of arms of the Lordship of Ireland

AH SURE IT'LL BE GRAND!

YOU'VE CHANGED SOMEWHAT, WILLIAM...

Norman Irish and Norman English

GOOD ✓

- ENGLISH LANGUAGE
- ENGLISH COMMON LAW
- ENGLISH SPORTS
- NO IRISH STORYTELLERS

BAD ✗

- IRISH LANGUAGE
- BREHON LAW
- IRISH SPORTS
- IRISH STORYTELLERS

1581 Gaelic Life

The Statutes of Kilkenny would attempt to erode the Brehon Laws. These laws defined much of Gaelic Irish life, which at the time focused quite a bit on social status. The laws, which dated back centuries, were interesting in that they were some of the only laws in Europe that frowned upon the death penalty, which was used only as a very, VERY last resort. The laws were more focused on fines and compensation for damage, theft or injury.

Like most people in Europe at the time, the Gaelic Irish and indeed the Irish Norman descendants and the English were Catholic, Christians of the Roman Catholic Church ruled from Rome, but soon that was about to change ...

A Gaelic Irish feast

1527 Henry VIII and The Reformation

In the 16th century, there was a movement in Europe against the Catholic Church. Some thought that the Church was too corrupt and not true to the teachings of Christ, so many, such as Martin Luther in Germany, split in protest, creating various Protestant Churches. This became known as the Reformation.

The English King Henry VIII wanted a son to carry on the great Tudor dynasty but his older wife Catherine of Aragon gave him a daughter, Mary. Henry was not pleased with this and spotted the much younger Anne Boleyn as a potential new wife. He wanted a divorce from Catherine, which was against the Catholic Church ... so he split from the Catholic Church and created his own Church, the Church of England.

SORRY DEAR BUT I JUST KNOW ME AND ANNE ARE MEANT TO LAST FOREVER!

Henry VIII rejects Catherine of Aragon for Anne Boleyn

······· DID YOU KNOW? ·······

Did you know? Henry VIII went through six wives trying to get a son: Catherine of Aragon (divorced), Anne Boleyn (beheaded), Jane Seymour (died), Anne of Cleves (divorced), Catherine Howard (beheaded), Catherine Parr (survived after his death). Three Catherines, two Annes and a Jane!

NO DIVORCE!!

FINE! I'LL JUST SE UP MY OWN CHURCH!

1542 The Kingdom of Ireland

Henry stripped the Catholic Church of its power across the British Isles, including Ireland, seizing their gold and treasures, destroying many monasteries and converting some Catholic cathedrals. The ruins of these monasteries can still be seen today across Ireland, a sad reminder of a troubled past. He reorganised Ireland into the Kingdom of Ireland, meaning that the King of England would also be the King of Ireland.

It was during this time that Ireland was divided up in 32 counties, Wicklow being the last to be formed in 1606.

These counties are still used today

1550s The Plantation of Laois and Offaly

GO LIVE THERE! IT'S OK, THEY'RE CATHOLIC!

After Henry VIII died his young son Edward became king but he was sickly and died at the age of 15. His half-sister Mary (daughter of Catherine of Aragon) became queen. She was strongly Catholic and tried to undo the Church of England reforms and executed many Protestants in the process, gaining the nickname 'Bloody Mary'.

OFFALY

LAOIS

This was a time of exploration across the world with the newly discovered continent of America being claimed by various European countries.

Mary decided to set up a plantation in King's County (Offaly) and Queen's County (Laois) in Ireland. A plantation was the taking of a small community from England and sending them to Ireland and planted there to set up a new community. Laois and Offaly were chosen because Gaelic Irish from there had been raiding The Pale, and they hoped the plantation would solve this problem. The English forces killed many of the opposing Gaelic Irish families but opposition was fierce. The plantation was ultimately a failure as the English settlers felt it was too dangerous living in such hostile conditions!

1590s The Plantation of Munster

GO LIVE THERE!

IT'S OK, THEY'RE ONLY CATHOLICS!

Mary died without an heir so the throne passed to her half-sister Elizabeth (daughter of Anne Boleyn). Elizabeth was strongly Protestant and a firm believer in the Church of England and under her rule she cemented the place of the Church of England as the main religion of England.

MUNSTER

In Ireland, some of the old Norman families didn't want so much control from England. They also remained Catholic after the Reformation, creating another rift. The Desmond dynasty of Munster led several rebellions but were defeated and their lands were confiscated. Elizabeth chose Munster to set up a new plantation and hopefully stabilise the area but, much like her sister's attempts, the plantation was a failure. The settlements were too spread out and not enough planters came over from England and Wales.

THAT'S NOT WHAT WE MEANT BY A HOUSE-WARMING PARTY!

Gráinne Mhaol
(Grace O'Malley)

Grace O'Malley (or Gráinne Mhaol, aka Granuaile) was a powerful woman in the west of Ireland. She had inherited her territory from her father who had been chieftain and with it a successful sea trade business. She demanded tolls off ships passing through her territory and sometimes took it by force, gaining a reputation as a pirate. As Queen Elizabeth was trying to tighten her hold over Ireland, Grace was a thorn in her side, putting up strong resistance and supporting other Gaelic chieftains fighting off the English invaders. Grace and Elizabeth actually met in Greenwich in London to discuss terms. Two formidable women of history! Grace spoke no English and Elizabeth spoke no Irish so they conversed in Latin. They came to an agreement that Elizabeth would pull her forces back from O'Malley's territory and in return, Grace would stop supporting the so-called rebels. Grace returned to Ireland but Elizabeth's forces ultimately returned, so Grace renewed her support of those opposing the English Crown.

1594-1603 Nine Years' War

ULSTER

SLIGO

NEWRY

WAYS INTO ULSTER!

The Province of Ulster. The symbol of the Red Hand of Ulster possibly comes from an old legend: the kingship of Ulster was to be decided by a boat race. Whoever's hand was first to touch the beach would become king. One of the losing competitors thought outside the box: he chopped off his hand and threw it to shore, winning him the kingship. The Red Hand and red streaks represent the blood and the yellow represents the beach.

In Elizabeth's last years, her forces fought the Nine Years' War against the chieftains of Ulster, Hugh O'Donnell and Hugh O'Neill, the last corner of open rebellion against her. Ulster had a strong defence; the only two clear ways for an army to get in was through Sligo or Newry. Everything in between was hills, forest and/or bog! Hugh O'Donnell hired Scottish mercenaries and both Hughs began gathering forces together. English advances were stopped initially and other parts of Ireland such as Munster rose up in rebellion too! The English forces were spread thin for a time but the men of Ulster couldn't hold out forever ...

Hugh O'Neill

Hugh O'Donnell

1601 The Battle of Kinsale

The Irish formed an alliance with Spain, an enemy of Britain and a fellow Catholic nation. They arranged for Spanish reinforcements to land but the Spanish landed on the wrong side of the country! O'Donnell and O'Neill marched all the way from Ulster to Cork where the Spanish were besieged in Kinsale by the English.

Poor communication and exhausted soldiers led to the battle being a complete disaster and the English were victorious. Hugh O'Donnell left Ireland and went to Spain where he would die. Hugh O'Neill surrendered a few years later only to find out that Queen Elizabeth had died a few weeks prior to the surrender. Thus ended the Nine Years' War lasting ... nine years.

Irish gallowglasses (heavy infantry) and kerns (light infantry) fighting English cavalry.

38

1607 The Flight of the Earls

IT'S OK LADS! YOUS CAN BE EARLS! JUST GIVE UP YOUR GAELIC TRADITIONS!

WHAT?

After Elizabeth I died without an heir, her cousin James, who was already the King of Scotland, became King of England. The new King James I went about doing things a little bit differently. Rather than punishing the rebels Rory O'Donnell (Hugh O'Donnell's nephew) and Hugh O'Neill, he made them earls. The earls soon discovered they had little real power and had to conform to English culture, abandoning the old Brehon Laws and Gaelic life. They were having none of it and decided to leave Ireland and return with an army to retake the country. They never returned, and the Flight of the Earls left Ireland up for grabs with no more Irish chieftains left. Hugh and Rory would ultimately die on a pilgrimage to Rome and are buried there.

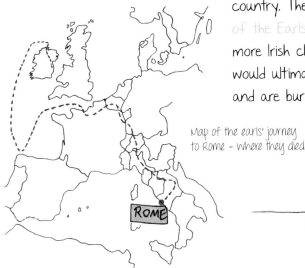

ROME

Map of the earls' journey to Rome - where they died

WE'LL BE BACK!

1609 The Plantation of Ulster

King James I of England,
James VI of Scotland

After the Flight of the Earls, the Gaelic Irish were left scattered, divided, leaderless. King James pressed this advantage and arranged the plantation of Ulster which was so successful that much of it still exists today (in the form of Northern Ireland). Part of its success came from its extensive network of towns and villages able to support each other in case of attack.

The old castle town of Derry was extensively refurbished and new walls were built that still stand today. The city was renamed Londonderry after the London guilds who established the new city.

Many plantation towns were built with a central triangular area or 'diamond' with roads leading out from each end. It meant the town couldn't be easily surrounded by an enemy and the people had the ability to flee or receive reinforcements from a nearby town. This layout can still be seen in many towns, especially in Ulster. Some of the best examples include Donegal town and Raphoe. This layout was later used in 1670 in Kenmare, County Kerry, by William Petty who mapped Ireland in the Down Survey.

Most planters from Scotland were Presbyterian while most planters from England were Church of England. This religious divide from the Catholic population would lead to bigger conflict in the 1640s!

NOTE ON RELIGIONS

CATHOLICISM The Gaelic Irish and old Norman Irish were mainly Catholic. The Catholic faith is ruled by the Roman Catholic Church from the Vatican in Rome. The Pope is the head of the Church and very powerful. Priests are not allowed to marry, and live as servants of God alone. At Mass it is believed that when the bread and wine are blessed for Communion, they actually become the Body and Blood of Christ. Masses were performed completely in Latin until the 1960s.

ANGLICANISM Followers of the Church of England are known as Anglicans. This was the faith established initially by Henry VIII and cemented by Elizabeth I. It replaced the Pope as head of the Church with the monarch, as it was their divine right by God to be king or queen. There is more of a focus on faith than prayers or Mass. Focus was brought back to Jesus, while Catholics had a whole legion of saints to pray to. In the Anglican faith, Christ becomes present within the bread and wine spiritually, rather than the bread and wine literally becoming the body and blood. When established in Ireland, their Church became known as the Church of Ireland.

PRESBYTERIANISM Based on the teachings of John Calvin, another reformed Protestant Church, Presbyterianism is much more democratic in how the congregation elects their elders. There is a strong focus on learning and studying scripture.

PRIVATELY PLANTED ALREADY

1641 Irish Confederate Wars

A religious movement in England was growing and it was called Puritanism. The Puritans were deeply religious and sought to reform the Church of England, rooting out the remnants of Catholic tradition and purifying it. They were growing weary of the King of England, Charles I, and believed he had too much power over Parliament. These growing tensions would lead to the English Civil War.

In Ireland, Catholics were worried that anti-Catholic forces would arrive from England so they staged a rebellion in 1641 but they were unable to take control. Ireland broke down into chaos and it turned into an ethnic conflict, Irish Catholics fighting against Scottish and English planters. Atrocities in Ulster were committed against the planters and whole villages of people were executed. In Portadown, villagers were forced at gunpoint to strip and jump into the icy river that November. Many drowned or were shot. In 1642 the Catholic Confederacy, ruled from Kilkenny, took control of the chaos but ethnic wars would continue throughout the decade while England was fighting its own civil war.

1649 Oliver Cromwell

Word of these massacres in Ulster reached England and people were appalled. A Puritan named Oliver Cromwell was leading the New Model Army against the Royalist English King's forces in the English Civil War. He led the Parliamentarians to victory and had King Charles I executed. After Cromwell was done settling things in England, he set his sights on Ireland.

The Execution of Charles I

Cromwell looks to Ireland

1649-1650 Cromwell in Ireland

In Ireland, Royalists (supporters of the English Crown) had allied themselves with the Catholic Confederates and awaited the arrival of Cromwell and his Parliamentarian forces. Cromwell landed and began capturing the ports along the east coast. The walled town of Drogheda was garrisoned by Royalist and Confederate forces so Cromwell laid siege and when the wall was breached, no quarter was given and the townspeople were massacred. In Wexford, too, Parliamentarian forces sacked the town while peace talks were going on. These atrocities were a double-edged sword. To some it showed what would happen if they resisted, but to others it showed what would happen to those who might've surrendered, so naturally resistance was fierce as Cromwell's forces swept across Ireland. The Royalist-Confederate Alliance collapsed when most of the Royalists went to fight alongside the Covenanters in Scotland. Cromwell returned to England in 1650 leaving his forces to defeat the army in Ulster and secure the island.

The Siege of Drogheda

1653 To Hell or To Connacht

Cromwell's campaign in Ireland left a path of death and destruction. There followed the largest land grab in Irish history in which the native Irish were ousted from their land and told to head west: 'To Hell or to Connacht'. Many women and children were sent across the Atlantic as indentured

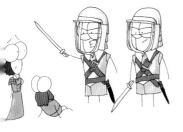

servants to the colonies in the Caribbean where they worked alongside enslaved Africans. This explains the slight Irish twang in some Caribbean accents today!

The English wanted control of all the best farmland in Ireland. They also controlled the coastline, ensuring the Irish didn't even have access to the sea.

Penal Laws were brought in to clamp down on Catholic and Presbyterian rights to conform to the Church of Ireland.

Cromwell ultimately became the Lord Protectorate until his death. After he died, his son wasn't as enthusiastic about politics and rule went back to King Charles II. Under his reign the Penal Laws initially were relaxed.

1688 The Williamite War

King Charles II died without any heirs so his brother became King James II. James had converted to Catholicism while in France and when this was discovered it made the predominantly Protestant English people uncomfortable to have a Catholic King. They were content enough, though, that James's Protestant daughter Mary would become queen ... until James's new young Catholic Italian wife gave birth to a boy, a new Catholic heir to the throne! Fearing for his family's lives James fled with them to France. The English people invited James's Dutch son-in-law William of Orange (husband of Mary) to be king. The complexities of Royal politics!!! This all became known as the Glorious Revolution in England.

Rejected King James II

WE DON'T WANT A CATHOLIC KING!

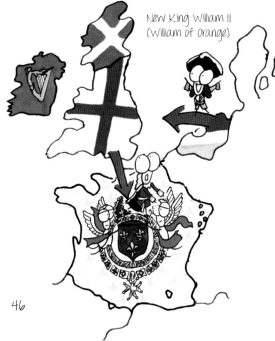

New King William III (William of Orange)

46

1689 The Siege of Derry

Exiled in France, James II stayed with his cousin, the French king. They decided the best way to retake England was to take Ireland first and gain Irish support. James had been supportive of Catholics in Ireland, allowing them into Parliament and even having a Catholic as Lord Deputy of Ireland. The supporters of James were known as the Jacobites. James landed in Ireland and secured Dublin. Williamite support was strongest in the north so James travelled with a French and Irish army to the city of Londonderry, a Protestant city not loyal to the Catholic King. The city shut their gates and were besieged throughout the winter. 'No Surrender!' was their cry. James's forces built a huge wooden boom across the River Foyle to stop Williamite ships reaching the city. William sent three ships to aid Londonderry and they managed to break the boom. They relieved the city and the siege was ended after 105 days and around 8,000 deaths.

1690 The Battle of the Boyne

A Williamite army landed in County Down and travelled south but was blocked at Dundalk and was stuck there throughout the winter. William of Orange himself grew impatient and landed in Belfast with over 30,000 troops. William was supported by many Protestant countries like Denmark and some German states but ironically William's cause was also backed by the Pope! The Pope didn't like the prospect of two powerful Catholic kings in alliance with each other so Rome made sure that didn't happen! William's forces marched south and met James's forces at Newry who retreated further south to the River Boyne. William's forces followed and it was there just outside of Drogheda that they fought the Battle of the Boyne! William's forces pushed across the river, forcing James's army to retreat. Although his army wasn't totally destroyed, James fled, leaving his army behind while he escaped to France!

Today the victory of William of Orange at the Boyne is celebrated in Northern Ireland and Scotland by the Orange Order on 12 July, though back then it was fought on 1 July. After the calendars were rearranged for the Gregorian calendar the anniversary landed on the 12th!

1 JULY WILL BE A DAY LONG REMEMBERED... PROVIDED THEY DON'T REARRANGE THE CALENDAR!

RUN AWAY!

48

1693 The Treaty of Limerick

HERE! HAVE ALL YOUR LAND BACK!

William of Orange marched to Dublin. Despite being abandoned by James, the Jacobites continued the fight and retreated to Limerick. They would hold the west for a time but after the Williamite victory at the Battle of Aughrim, the Jacobites ultimately surrendered in Limerick. William struck a sweet deal with the Catholics, giving them their land back and freedom of religion in the Treaty of Limerick. The mainly Protestant Parliament in Dublin

YEA, SO I GAVE THE CATHOLICS THEIR LAND BACK.

UM YOU CAN'T REALLY DO THAT...

wouldn't ratify the Treaty and brought back the Penal Laws to clamp down on Catholic rights and have Ireland conform to the Church of Ireland. Clergy could be executed on sight and had to practise Mass in secret at Mass rocks. Presbyterians also were oppressed by the Penal Laws.

PENAL LAWS

CONFORM TO THE CHURCH OF IRELAND!

MASS IS ILLEGAL?

YEA, YOU KINDA HAVE TO GET OUT OF THE COUNTRY!

1700s The Ascendancy

The Penal Laws resulted in the emergence of a Protestant ruling class that became known as the Protestant Ascendancy. The Laws excluded Catholics and Presbyterians from Parliament resulting in the decision-making being done by the Church of Ireland Anglo-Irish. The many rebellions, wars and defeats over the centuries resulted in more and more land being confiscated by the English and given to someone considered more loyal. As a result by the start of the 18th century, Catholic land ownership was hugely reduced, despite them being the majority of the population. The difficulty for Catholic landowners too was their old tradition of land inheritance resulted in the division of land amongst the heirs so farms would get smaller and less profitable. The Anglo-Irish usually passed their land onto the eldest boy, resulting in large estates being maintained. Catholics living on these estates paid rent to the landlord.

■ 0-24% CATHOLIC LAND OWNERSHIP
■ 25-49% CATHOLIC LAND OWNERSHIP
☐ 50-100% CATHOLIC LAND OWNERSHIP

1641 ⟹ 1703 (POST CROMWELL

The change of land ownership between 1641 and 1703

The 'Big House' came to represent the Protestant Ascendancy in the minds of the Irish

Georgian Dublin

It was during this time that Dublin was developed into one of the finest cities on the British Isles. The architectural style at the time known as Georgian because the various English kings of England at the time were named George. It's similar to the Georgian architecture found in London.

GPO 1818

CUSTOM HOUSE 1791

HOUSES OF PARLIAMENT
(NOW BANK OF IRELAND)
1739 – 1787

FITZWILLIAM
SQUARE 1792

1790s Revolutionary Times

The Penal Laws effectively united Catholics and Presbyterians against the English because they weren't allowed to practise their religion openly, in favour of the Church of England. The end of the 18th century was a time of Revolution! The colonies in America rebelled and defeated the British and formed the United States of America in 1776. The people of France rose up against their king, executing him and establishing a new regime. Both the USA and France set out to establish a Republic, a system of government where every person has representation, not just the rich or the clergy.

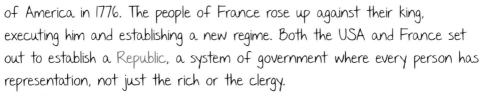

At this time a new Society was growing: the United Irishmen. This was a group of mainly Presbyterians and some Anglicans who believed Catholics and Protestants should be united together in a Republic independent of Britain.

VIVE LA RÉVOLUTION!

The British government obviously didn't like this so they fuelled the newly formed Orange Order with sectarian fears and rumours of Catholic attacks. They took the divide-and-conquer approach, keeping Catholics and Protestants on opposing sides, ensuring the people of Ireland would never be united. Sectarian violence grew and harsh martial law was bringing pitch-capping, torture and murder to the people.

The United Irishmen began to plan a rebellion and their leader Theobald Wolfe Tone travelled to France to muster an army. At that time revolutionary France was at war with half of Europe, including Great Britain!

Pitch-capping used hot pitch applied to the head - not pleasant.

1798 The 1798 Rebellion

Theobald Wolfe Tone was a young Anglican politician who helped set up the United Irishmen. He is known as the father of Irish Republicanism. Throughout the 1790s Britain was at war with revolutionary France. Wolfe Tone saw this as an opportunity to get support from France. In 1796 Tone attempted to land 14,000 French troops in Bantry but the ships were unable to land due to fierce storms.

By 1798, civil unrest was growing and the United Irishmen decided they couldn't wait for Wolfe Tone and the French. They must do something now! In May, they planned to begin their rebellion in Dublin, and the surrounding counties would rise and prevent reinforcements entering the city.

The Battle of Vinegar Hill

British forces, however, were informed shortly before and they were ready for the rebels in Dublin, arresting them, including many of the leaders. The surrounding counties rose up with hard fighting in Kildare, Armagh, Wicklow and especially Wexford where the rebels held the county until they were defeated at the Battle of Vinegar Hill. The rebellion was crushed and swept up by July. Meanwhile Wolfe Tone was organising the French reinforcements ...

Wolfe Tone had been in France fighting in their revolutionary army against the rest of Europe, while trying to convince them to send a force to Ireland. Unfortunately by the time the French made moves in August, the Irish rebellion had been quelled. A small force did land in Killala Bay, County Mayo, but were defeated by British forces. Wolfe Tone himself arrived in October where he fought a naval battle off the coast of Tory Island. His ship was captured and he was taken to Buncrana in County Donegal where he was arrested. Wolfe Tone was to be executed. He was refused a soldier's death by firing squad and would face a traitor's death by hanging. While awaiting the execution, Wolfe Tone cut his own throat. He died but the idea of an Irish Republic would not.

1801 Acts of Union

After the Rebellion, the Parliament in Dublin was dissolved, and Ireland was to be ruled directly from the Parliament in London. In Britain's eyes, Irish rebels had allied with France with whom Britain was at war and thus were not to be trusted. The Dublin Parliament didn't like this ... until they were bribed. Ireland merged with Great Britain to form the United Kingdom of Great Britain and Ireland in the Acts of Union.

St Patrick's Saltire was integrated into the British flag to create the Union Flag still used today. (It should only be referred to as the Union Jack when it's on a ship!)

Because all the decisions were now being made in London, many landlords left Ireland and much of the wealth earned on the land was now being exported, which would lead to catastrophic problems in the not-too-distant future!

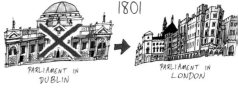

1829 Catholic Emancipation

One positive thing to emerge from the early 19th century was Catholic Emancipation: Irish Catholics regained many of their rights and the ability to become Members of Parliament.

Daniel O'Connell

GOD I'M GREAT!

AT LEAST HE'S MODEST...

An Orange Order march

The Roman Catholic Relief Act 1829 was fronted by Kerry-born politician Daniel O'Connell who travelled the country gaining support, Ireland at this point being around 85 per cent Catholic. The Protestants of the North were not too happy about emancipation and continued their Orange marches.

O'Connell was a very charismatic man and became loved by many in Ireland. King George IV even complained that it seemed like O'Connell was the King of Ireland! Daniel O'Connell went on to become Lord Mayor of Dublin, the first Catholic to do so in centuries. Today one of the largest streets in Dublin is named after O'Connell, where his statue stands looking across the Liffey.

1845-1852 The Great Famine

The poor Catholic farmers had grown dependent on the potato for food. It was cheap and easy to grow! During the 1840s, a disease called potato blight spread across Europe and turned potatoes into stinking inedible mulch. The blight reached Ireland in 1845 and whole crops were lost. The next year, was no better. Hunger and disease spread across the land, and 1847 was so bad it is known as Black '47. Millions died of starvation and disease.

The word 'famine' is actually inaccurate as it was only the potatoes that failed. Other grain crops (wheat, oats, barley) and livestock were plentiful but they were for exporting, not eating! Some landlords cruelly cared little for their starving tenants, if indeed the landlords were even there; others were more merciful. Some landlords nearly bankrupted themselves trying to feed their tenants.

1845–1890s and beyond Emigration

Many poor farmers left Ireland for England to work in cities. Some got on 'coffin ships' to America. They were known as coffins ships because not everyone survived the journey across the Atlantic. They would come into places like New York or Boston, working wherever they could, brushing up against countless other nationalities, all there to start a new life.

Some of those who were starving in Ireland dared to steal the corn to eat and for that they were shipped away as criminals to the other side of the world to the penal colonies in Australia.

Ever since the Famine, in times of hardship, emigration has been an answer. Throughout the 20th and 21st centuries, in times of economic struggle, waves of young Irish people have left to find work elsewhere.

Before the Famine, Ireland's population was around 8 million. By the end of the 19th century, it was 1 million. Ireland's population has never since reached 8 million.

Irish Republicanism

Robert Emmet

There was huge anger in the wake of the Famine and many Irish blamed the British government. Many believed that it was allowed happen, that poor Irish Catholics were allowed to die or leave: ethnic cleansing by neglect. The idea of an Irish Republic had

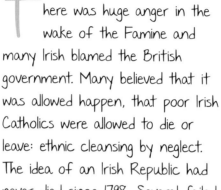

HOW COULD THIS BE LET HAPPEN?

never died since 1798. Several failed rebellions had sprung up since then, such as Robert Emmet's rebellion in Dublin in 1803. In 1848, the Young Irelanders unveiled the Irish tricolour in Waterford. It was based on the French Republic's tricolour. Green represented the Republican movement, and was used by the United Irishmen, orange represented the Protestant North who supported the Union with Great Britain, and white symbolised a lasting peace between the two. The flag was an invitation for all to be a part of a new united Irish Republic.

CÚCHULAINN
2000 BCE
(MYTHOLOGY)

THEOBALD WOLFE TONE
1798

ROBERT EMMET
1803

20th-century republican P.H. Pearse inspired by fallen heroes

In 1858, with the effects of the Famine still raw, the Irish Republican Brotherhood (IRB) was founded by James Stephens in America. At that point, there were more and more Irish people in America than in Ireland. The

ERIN GO BRAGH!

James Stephens

IRISH REPUBLICAN BROTHERHOOD
I.R.B.

Fenian Brotherhood was also founded there that same year and would provide a nickname for the whole Republican movement: 'Fenians'.

Thomas Clarke

Jeremiah O'Donovan Rossa

The IRB was a secret revolutionary organisation that sought to set up an Irish Republic by force. One Fenian in particular, Jeremiah O'Donovan Rossa, believed that newly invented dynamite could wake up Britain. IRB members would be trained how to use it in the USA and O'Donovan Rossa would send them back across the Atlantic. He organised the Dynamite Campaign, a series of terrorist bombings across English cities throughout the 1880s. One young man who was arrested for taking part in these bombings was Thomas Clarke, and we'll see him later!

1880s-1890s The Gaelic Revival

While Republican movements were underground, a cultural revolution was taking place! The culture of Ireland was becoming anglicised, becoming more British, with old traditions, stories, sports and even the Irish language falling out of fashion. In the late 19th century an interest in Gaelic culture sparked the Gaelic Revival!

original GAA crest

The Gaelic Athletic Association was set up in 1884 to promote the playing of old Irish sports like Gaelic football, hurling, handball, camogie and rounders. The game of hurling is indeed a very ancient sport, being mentioned in ancient Celtic mythology. It is one of the fastest ball sports in the world!

Irish dancing and traditional music took a big boost. Traditional Irish instruments include the fiddle, the flute, the tin whistle, bodhrán, the uileann pipes and, of course, the harp, a symbol of Ireland for centuries.

By the end of the 19th century the Irish language was dying. There were more Irish speakers living in America than there were in Ireland! Children were taught through English and the Irish language was often literally beaten out of them!

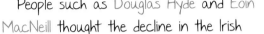

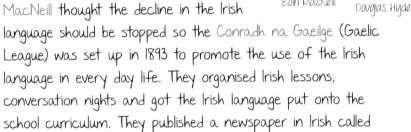

People such as Douglas Hyde and Eoin MacNeill thought the decline in the Irish language should be stopped so the Conradh na Gaeilge (Gaelic League) was set up in 1893 to promote the use of the Irish language in every day life. They organised Irish lessons, conversation nights and got the Irish language put onto the school curriculum. They published a newspaper in Irish called An Claidheamh Soluis (The Sword of Light).

Eoin MacNeill

Douglas Hyde

Crest of Conradh na Gaeilge

The GAA and Conradh na Gaeilge are still in existence today in Ireland!

Ireland also gained a national theatre: the Abbey Theatre, set up by writers such as W. B. Yeats, J. M. Synge and Lady Gregory in 1904.

All of these movements helped grow a sense of Irish identity that was being lost. Irish Nationalism was on the rise!

W. B. Yeats

USEFUL IRISH PHRASES:

Dia dhuit – Hello

Conas atá tú? – How are you?

Tá mé go maith! – I am well!

Go raibh maith agat – Thank you

Fáilte romhat – You're welcome

An bhfuil cead agam dul go dtí an leithreas?
– Can I go to the toilet?

63

1870s-1890s Home Rule

WE WANT HOME RULE!

Isaac Butt

Amidst this rise of Nationalism, the demand for a parliament back in Dublin was growing. The people wanted Home Rule! Donegal politician Isaac Butt set up the Home Rule League in 1873, a political party to push for Home Rule. This went on to become the Irish Parliamentary Party under Charles Stewart Parnell. Parnell was also involved in the Land League, which was founded by Michael Davitt to allow tenant farmers to buy the land they worked or at least get fairer rent, especially if the landlord wasn't even in the country! They organised huge 'monster meetings' across the country to unite people in their thousands against the landlords. While the IRB was trying to gain Irish independence through violence, the Irish Parliamentary Party sought to do it through Parliament, through Home Rule.

WE WANT **HOME RULE**!!!

Charles Stewart Parnell

Westminster Parliament in London

1912 The Ulster Covenant

HOME RULE?
ROME RULE!!

LOL!

Demand for Home Rule grew in Ireland, except in the Protestant North. The majority of the Protestants in Ulster were Unionist, supporting the Union with Britain. Industry was going strong for them with Belfast being the largest city in Ireland at the start of the 20th century. They believed that a parliament in Dublin would be run by the Catholic Church so thousands signed the Ulster Covenant led by Edward Carson and James Craig, threatening open war against the South if Home Rule was passed.

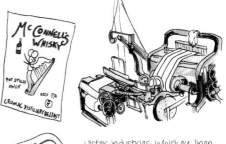

Ulster industries: whiskey, linen, tobacco, shipbuilding

The signing of the Ulster Covenant in Belfast City Hall

1913 The Home Rule Crisis

IRISH VOLUNTEERS

ULSTER VOLUNTEERS

To defend their loyalty to Britain the Unionists set up the Ulster Volunteers. They smuggled rifles from Germany into Larne, County Antrim, and began arming the people. In reaction to this, Irish Nationalists in the South formed the Irish Volunteers and they too ran guns into Howth just north of Dublin. Tensions were running high and Ireland was on the brink of civil war. If Home Rule was passed, the Ulster Volunteers would go to war.

WE'RE NOT GONNA FIGHT THE VOLUNTEERS!

Poster for Home Rule

DID YOU KNOW?

The Curragh Mutiny happened at this time, when Irish soldiers in the Curragh Army Camp, County Kildare, protested because they were potentially going to have to go to war against the Ulster Volunteers when Home Rule came in. The soldiers didn't like the idea of going to war against their fellow countrymen!

1913 Dublin Lock-Out

THE GREAT APPEAR GREAT BECAUSE WE ARE ON OUR KNEES! LET US RISE!!

MURPHY MUST GO!

DON'T WEAR CLOTHES MADE BY SCAB LABOUR!

'Big Jim' Larkin

Liberty Hall

WE SERVE NEITHER KING NOR KAISER BUT IRELAND

Irish Citizen Army

James Connolly

The Plough and the Stars

Meanwhile, Dublin had some of the poorest living conditions in Europe. Many poor families lived in cramped conditions in tenement buildings. There was an incident where one of these tenement buildings collapsed because the people had removed the floorboards for firewood. Unskilled dockworkers were at the mercy of their employers. Any talk of coming together or unionising could get you blacklisted and not get any more work! A man called James Larkin stood up and helped them form a union. Together, he and James Connolly set up the Labour Party as Home Rule began to approach. Larkin and Connolly would lead the workers on strike to demand better pay and working conditions. In August 1913, 300 employers locked out 20,000 Dublin workers and brought in workers from elsewhere, leaving the poor people of Dublin with no income to feed their families. During protests, the Dublin Metropolitan Police weren't too gentle with the protesters so James Connolly set up the Irish Citizen Army to protect them. The lock-out ended in January 1914 in defeat: the poor people went back to work promising not to unionise.

1914 The Great War

In 1914 Home Rule was voted into the British Parliament ... but in June, a gang of Serbians shot the Austro-Hungarian Archduke Franz Ferdinand in Sarajevo (1), so Austria-Hungary went to war with Serbia (2) so Russia went to war with Austria-Hungary to defend Serbia (3), so Germany went to war with Russia (4). Knowing that France would defend Russia, Germany pre-emptively went to war with France via neutral Belgium and Luxembourg (5) so Great Britain stepped in to defend Belgium (6). Ultimately all the imperial colonies around the world were brought in to fight and the First World War began!

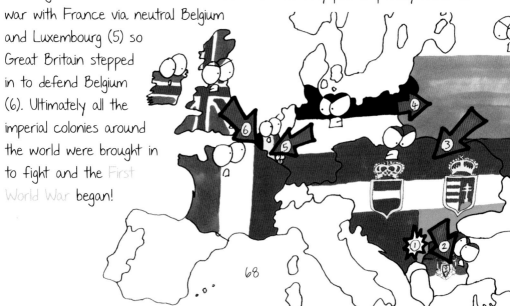

UM YEA... HOME RULE WILL HAVE TO WAIT.

OK...

Life in the trenches

Home Rule was suspended while Britain fought the war with many Irishmen heading off to fight in the trenches. Many people thought the war would be over by Christmas (it would actually drag on for four years). Irish Parliamentary Party leader John Redmond encouraged men to join the army. It was an opportunity for them to get trained and get experience from one of the greatest armies in the world and return as an army for an independent Ireland. What they didn't know was the horror and carnage that awaited them in the trenches of France and Belgium.

HOME RULE WILL BE WAITING FOR YOU WHEN YOU GET HOME!

John Redmond

NOW IS THE TIME TO STRIKE!!

There was a split in the Irish Volunteers. Some agreed to join the British Army and fight in the trenches, others believed now was the time to strike!

WE'LL COME BACK STRONGER!

Road to the Rising

Thomas Clarke

Patrick Pearse

Jeremiah
O'Donovan
Rossa

The IRB had been working away behind the scenes. Thomas Clarke chose Patrick Pearse to be the new younger face of the Irish Republican movement. Pearse was a teacher and a poet from Dublin. He took great inspiration from mythical hero Cúchulainn and other fallen Republican leaders such as Wolfe Tone and Robert Emmet. Jeremiah O'Donovan Rossa's funeral in 1915 drew a huge crowd of Republicans to Glasnevin cemetery in Dublin. Pearse gave a rousing graveside oration, famously saying (referring to Britain) 'The fools! The fools! The fools! They have left us our Fenian dead! And while Ireland holds these graves, Ireland unfree shall never be at peace!' A new spark was lit in younger Republicans.

IRELAND UNFREE SHALL NEVER BE AT PEACE!!

THAT'S OUR MAN!

1915

Seán MacDiarmada

Thomas MacDonagh

Éamonn Ceannt

Joseph Mary Plunkett

Clarke, Pearse and other IRB leaders planned to stage a rebellion on Easter Sunday 1916, a symbolic day of resurrection and new life. The other leaders included Seán MacDiarmada, a young politician from County Leitrim; Thomas MacDonagh, a university lecturer from County Tipperary; Éamonn Ceannt, a piper and member of Conradh na Gaeilge from County Galway; and Joseph Mary Plunkett, a poet and journalist from Dublin.

In protest against the imperialist war in Europe, James Connolly had hung a banner outside Liberty Hall: 'We serve neither King nor Kaiser but Ireland!' Connolly and his Citizens' Army threatened to fight the British themselves, believing the Republicans were all talk. The IRB quickly brought him into the fold before he did something rash and destroyed all their plans.

CUMANN NA MBAN
(THE IRISHWOMEN'S COUNCIL)

At that time, women did not have the right to vote, let alone many other liberties. Cumann na mBan (The Women's League), who were akin to the suffragette movement, also joined the planned rebellion. They believed a Republic would be a great way to achieve equal rights for women!

1915 Plans for the Rising

WE'LL GIVE YOU 20,000 RUSSIAN RIFLES, SOME MACHINE GUNS AND SOME AMMO. GUT, NE?

Roger Casement

The top-secret plan was that the Volunteers were to march throughout the country on Easter Sunday and when the signal was given they would capture important spots and hold the country. The British would be caught unawares while they were waging war in Europe. Roger Casement was in Germany trying to secure aid for the Rising. They couldn't spare troops but sent weapons to be landed near Tralee Bay. The British found out, however. Casement was arrested and the weapons never made it to the rebels.

Eoin MacNeill, who was in charge of the Irish Volunteers, thought it was crazy to go up against the might of the British Army. Because of this, he'd been kept in the dark about the Rising but when he found out about the plans and Casement's failed weapons landing, he issued a countermanding order around the country the day before Easter Sunday! It ordered all Volunteers not to take part in any marches, movements, or parades, so it seemed as if the Rising was off!

NO VOLUNTEER PARADES!

Eoin MacNeill, Chief of Staff of the Irish Volunteers

OH NEIN!!

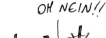

SS 'Libau' disguised as Norwegian ship 'Aud'

1916 The Proclamation

The Rising leaders had an emergency meeting and decided to postpone the Rising for a day and make their move on Easter Monday at noon! Because they couldn't spread this message around the country fast enough at such short notice, the Rising would mainly be focused around Dublin with a few pockets of resistance elsewhere.

The seven leaders, acting as the Provisional Government for the Irish Republic, drafted up and signed the Proclamation of Independence, a document outlining the Republic that they wanted to establish for Ireland, guaranteeing 'religious and civil liberty, equal rights and equal opportunities to all its citizens' and declaring 'its resolve to pursue the happiness and prosperity of the whole nation and of all its parts, cherishing all the children of the nation equally'.

They signed it and sent it to the printers for the big day. They had a busy week ahead!

1916 The Easter Rising

The Irish Volunteers and Citizens Army came together on Easter Monday and captured the General Post Office on Sackville Street. Volunteers across the city captured other locations such as the Four Courts, the Jacob's factory, Boland's Mills and the South Dublin Union. The idea was to keep British soldiers out of the city for as long as possible, all the barracks being on the outskirts.

At 12.45 p.m. Pearse stepped out in front of the GPO and read the Proclamation to a fairly small, quiet and confused crowd. Most of the poor Dubliners didn't care about the politics but as law and order broke down they began looting the shops!

IRISHMEN AND IRISH WOMEN!! IN THE NAME OF GOD AND OF THE DEAD GENERATIONS FROM WHICH SHE RECEIVES HER OLD TRADITION OF NATIONHOOD, IRELAND, THROUGH US, SUMMONS HER CHILDREN TO HER FLAG AND STRIKES FOR HER FREEDOM!!

TUE 25 APRIL

LONG LIVE THE IRISH REPUBLIC OR WHATEVER!

SUGAR

British reinforcements arrived from Belfast, Athlone and the Curragh on Tuesday. By Wednesday they had set up artillery pointed at the rebels. Connolly thought the British would never shell their own buildings ... he was wrong! More reinforcements arrived from England but were caught in a deadly trap as they tried to enter the city at Mount Street Bridge. Seven rebels shot dead 24 British soldiers while wounding over 200 others!

Connolly was hit by a ricocheting bullet on Thursday, and had to be put on a stretcher. By Friday, Sackville Street was a blazing inferno and the rebels had to evacuate the GPO and make their way to Moore Street.

Howitzer guns set up in front of Trinity College

Sackville Street in flames

THU 27 APRIL

James Connolly hit by a bullet

75

1916 Surrender and Executions

The civilian death toll was ever growing. Many innocent people were killed in the crossfire. Out of 466 deaths in the Rising, 254 were civilian, with thousands more injured.

The rebels burrowed their way through the buildings of Moore Street, but as the civilian death toll rose, Pearse and the leaders decided to surrender. Elizabeth O'Farrell was sent out with a white flag and Pearse ultimately surrendered.

FRI 28 APRIL

THIS IS NO.16 ISN'T IT?

PLUNKET

Rebels burrowing through the buildings of Moore Street

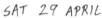
SAT 29 APRIL

The ruins of Dublin

SAT 29 APRIL

I ACCEPT YOUR OFFER OF UNCONDITIONAL SURRENDER

Pearse surrendering to General Lowe

SERIOUSLY? NOW IS THE TIME YOU CHOOSE TO LIGHT A CIGARETTE?

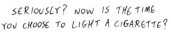

The positions across Dublin eventually stood down and the rebels were rounded up. General Maxwell, who was in charge of the British forces in Ireland, promptly had the leaders court-martialled and the executions began in Kilmainham Gaol less than a week after the surrender. Pearse was executed on the first day, Connolly on the last. Connolly was unable to stand because of his badly infected leg so they strapped him to a chair and shot him all the same.

Maxwell thought he was setting an example; what he was actually doing was making martyrs! Éamon de Valera, Constance Markievicz and William T. Cosgrave avoided execution.

TUE 2 MAY

A RATHER CUNNING PLAN SIR!

WE WILL EXECUTE THESE REBEL SCUM!

GENERAL CHARLES BLACKADER

GENERAL SIR JOHN MAXWELL

KILMAINHAM GAOL

The men who were executed in May 1916 for the Easter Rising: (l-r) Patrick Pearse, Thomas Clarke, Thomas MacDonagh, Edward 'Ned' Daly, Willie Pearse, Michael O'Hanrahan, Joseph Plunkett, John MacBride, Seán Heuston, Michael Mallin, Éamonn Ceannt, Con Colbert, Seán MacDiarmada, James Connolly

1916 A Terrible Beauty Is Born

During the Rising, the rebels had little support from the general public. Dublin was lying in rubble and people were angry at the needless death and destruction. The executions suddenly began to strike a chord with the people. They saw the ruthlessness of British justice and began to realise it wasn't the rebels who did the shelling! The idea of an Irish Republic grew ever quicker in the hearts of the people of Ireland. The Irish Volunteers were reorganised as the Irish Republican Army (IRA). By the time the World War ended in 1918, Ireland was a changed place. Soldiers who were cheered off as they went to war were shunned when they returned, if indeed they returned!

The 1918 General Election saw a landslide victory for the Irish Republican party Sinn Féin (We Ourselves). Ireland wanted a Republic!

1918

BRITISH PARLIAMENT
ELECTION RESULTS

SINN FÉIN

IRISH UNIONISTS

IRISH PARLIAMENTARY PARTY

LABOUR UNIONISTS

1919-1921 The War of Independence

In early 1919 the elected officials of Sinn Féin (whoever wasn't in jail or on the run) chose not to take their seats in London and instead met in the Mansion House in Dublin, establishing the Irish Parliament – Dáil Éireann – and declared Irish independence. The IRA were quick to start a violent campaign against British forces in Ireland, using guerrilla tactics such as ambushes and assassinations.

WE DECLARE INDEPENDENCE!!

Mansion House, Dublin

The leaders, such as Michael Collins and Éamon de Valera, who had fought in the Easter Rising, went into hiding. The British sent reinforcements in the form of the Black and Tans (nicknamed for the colour of their uniform) and the Auxiliaries. Both became known for their violence and vengeance, sometimes against innocent civilians. The violence was centred mainly on Cork, Dublin and Belfast.

Michael Collins

Éamon de Valera

1921-1922 A Truce and A Treaty

The day 21 November 1920 became known as Bloody Sunday. In the morning, Michael Collins had an entire British spy network assassinated. In revenge, the Auxiliaries opened fire on the crowd at a football match in Croke Park, killing 14 people and wounding over 60 others.

The fighting ultimately ended in a stalemate when the British called for a truce in July 1921. Over 2,000 people had been killed in the conflict. The British wanted to negotiate!

LADS, IT'S AN AWFUL LOT OF PAPERWORK!

During the fighting, Unionists in the North knew that, no matter the outcome, they wanted to remain part of Britain. Because of this, the British government made provisions and six counties of Ulster became partitioned from the rest of the island, becoming Northern Ireland in 1921.

Those counties were Derry, Antrim, Down, Armagh, Tyrone and Fermanagh.

Michael Collins and Arthur Griffith travelled to England to enter into negotiations with British Prime Minister David Lloyd George and a whole team of negotiators. From it came the Anglo-Irish Treaty, which created the 26-county Irish Free State.

NORTHERN IRELAN

The Free State would be a dominion of the British Empire, similar to Canada and Australia. The English King would still be head of state and the Irish government would have to pledge the Oath of Allegiance to the Crown. Three Irish ports would be held by the British Navy: Lough Swilly in County Donegal, and Berehaven and Spike Island in County Cork.

CONSTITUTION OF THE FREE STATE OF IRELAND [English Translation]

dá ping inn TWOPENCE

The Treaty also allowed Northern Ireland to opt out of joining the Free State, cementing partition to this day.

The Treaty was ratified and the Dáil voted in favour of it by 64 to 57 votes, but seeing it as a betrayal to the Irish Republic, Éamon de Valera, leader of Sinn Féin, left the Dáil in protest along with his supporters. Michael Collins and his supporters believed that the Free State would be a stepping stone to complete independence, giving them 'the freedom to achieve freedom'. The 1922 general election showed more support for Pro-Treaty Sinn Féin but de Valera wouldn't accept this. Neither side would budge on the matter and the Civil War began!

NO IRISH FREE STATE!! WE WANT A REPUBLIC!!

Michael Collins

FREE STATE!!!!

REPUBLIC!!!!

The Civil War was bitter. It put former comrades against each other, sometimes dividing families.

The IRA was divided into those who opposed the Treaty and remained the IRA and those who supported the Treaty and became the National Army, now armed by Britain. As British control was handed over to the Irish, Pro-Treaty and Anti-Treaty groups took control across the country. The IRA occupied the Four Courts in Dublin to force British intervention and unite the Irish once more, but Collins wanted to make the Free State work. He was hesitant to fire upon the IRA but with growing pressure from Britain, Collins began shelling the Four Courts. After fierce fighting in the streets of Dublin, the Free Staters took control of the capital.

Republican support was strong outside the capital especially in the west and south, the south earning the nickname 'The Munster Republic'. But as much as there was support, the Free State National Army was too well armed for the IRA who slowly fell to Free State forces. While visiting his home county, Michael Collins was killed in a Republican ambush at Béal na Bláth, August 1922.

UP THE REPUBLIC!!

Both sides briefly stopped to mourn Collins but the war soon descended into bitter attacks and revenge. The IRA burned Free State homes as well as old Anglo-Irish and Loyalist homes; Free Staters ruthlessly executed Republicans. It has still left a dark memory on Irish politics today. Ultimately, in May 1923, the Republicans surrendered, their cause seemingly hopeless against the National Army. Republicans were arrested and imprisoned for a time. The general election of 1923 saw more support for newly formed Pro-Treaty party Cumann na nGaedheal (which would become Fine Gael in 1933). De Valera, now released, decided to reform the Free State from within and established the party Fianna Fáil in 1924. Fine Gael and Fianna Fáil would dominate Irish politics and oppose each other in government until they both failed to win a majority in the general election of 2016 when they formed a government together.

Fianna Fáil

Fine Gael

1922-1937 The Free State

The Civil War had cost Ireland greatly, both in lives and money. Life was tough economically for the early Irish Free State but it trudged on. As leader of Cumann na nGaedheal, W. T. Cosgrave was the President of the Executive Council, with Éamon de Valera in opposition. The new Irish police force, An Garda Síochána (Guardian of Peace), was set up in 1923.

W. T. Cosgrave

In 1932, Fianna Fáil won the general election and de Valera became leader of the government. With memories still raw from the Civil War, politicians brought guns with them just in case but the change of power happened peacefully.

THIS SALUTE IS TOTALLY GONNA BE FASHIONABLE FOREVER!!

Many IRA prisoners were released at this time and the fascist group known as the Blueshirts were set up to defend members of Cumann na nGaedheal. De Valera spent the next ten years dismantling the Free State from the inside (which was what Michael Collins had suggested before the Civil War ...). He began with getting rid of the Oath of Allegiance to the Crown and creating a new constitution. It ended the Irish Free State and the country would be known as Ireland (or Éire in Irish). The position of the President of Ireland was created, the first being Douglas Hyde. The Prime Minister of Ireland would be known as Taoiseach (Irish for Chieftain) from now on. The Treaty Ports were also returned to Ireland, and in good time! War was looming in Europe!

BUNREACHT NA hÉIREANN
CONSTITUTION OF IRELAND

1939-1945 The 'Emergency'

When the Second World War broke out across Europe, Ireland was able to remain neutral: de Valera was not yet ready to fight beside Britain! Dublin was accidentally bombed by Germany but Ireland stayed out nonetheless. Huge stone signs saying 'EIRE' visible from the air were built up and down the west coast to inform pilots they were flying over neutral territory.

With Northern Ireland still being part of the UK, Belfast suffered German air raids. The white parliament building in Stormont was actually painted brown, using a mixture of paint and cow manure, to hide it from German bombers. The cow manure was used so they could scrub it off again, and it worked ... mostly. Lough Erne in County Fermanagh was used as an airbase. It was really close to the Atlantic but was blocked by neutral Irish airspace so they'd have to fly all the way around Donegal ... unless Ireland just let them through ... which they did ... Irish neutrality indeed!

YEA... WE'RE GONNA SIT THIS ONE OUT...

1940s

I GUESS IRELAND WILL LOOK LOVELY AT NIGHT.

EIRE

ORIGINAL ROUTE TO THE ATLANTIC

SHORTCUT

— AH SURE IT'LL BE GRAND!

1948 The Republic

YAY! WE'RE A REPUBLIC!!

In 1948 Ireland officially became the Republic of Ireland, recognising the President of Ireland as the head of state, officially replacing the King of England. Ireland was no longer part of the British Commonwealth.

Ireland had strong links with the USA due to the generations of emigrants living there. The 1960s saw one of their descendants, John F. Kennedy, becoming President of the United States, their first Catholic President. JFK visited Ireland in 1963, months before his assassination. Irish pride grew despite tough economic times.

John F. Kennedy

With the 50th anniversary of the Easter Rising in 1966 came great celebration but also a sense of a job unfinished, with the North still under British control. The IRA, an underground movement once more, blew up Nelson's Pillar in Dublin, a symbol of British rule. Protestants in the North grew weary.

The North/South divide in Ireland led to very strong identity politics, Protestants in the North, Catholics in the South. The Republic became a very Catholic state, the 1937 Constitution recognising the Catholic Church's 'special place' in society. The Church had a lot of influence in running the country and the laws that were made, and people did not dare to criticise!

1960s Civil Rights in the North

Northern Ireland was established as 'a Protestant State for a Protestant people', despite roughly a third of the population being Catholic. The Catholics in the North had been greatly discriminated against since the state's foundation, finding it difficult to get jobs and even decent housing.

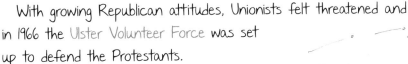

With growing Republican attitudes, Unionists felt threatened and in 1966 the Ulster Volunteer Force was set up to defend the Protestants.

Seeing the Civil Rights movement for African Americans in the US in the 1960s, many Catholics and liberal Protestants decided to march for equal rights for Catholics in the North. The marches started out as peaceful but heavy-handed policing by the Protestant police, the B-Specials, resulted in violence from both sides. The riots increased in intensity and chaos ensued. In August 1969, the British Army was called in as peacekeepers between the Catholics and Protestants, which initially brought an end to the riots ... but it was not to last!

1970s-1980s The Troubles

TIOCFAIDH ÁR LÁ!

The IRA declared their right to use force against a foreign army on Irish soil. They began a campaign of bombings, shootings and other terrorist tactics to fight what they saw as the British occupation. The Unionist groups UVF and the UDA (Ulster Defence Association) carried out similar attacks on Catholic targets. Amidst the violence many civilians were killed.

To counter the terrorism, internment without trial was introduced, meaning British forces could imprison anyone suspected of being involved with the IRA! Many who were interned were not involved, but their harsh treatment certainly changed some minds and they joined the IRA upon release!

YOU ARE NOW ENTERING FREE DERRY

The Bogside in Derry was a particularly Republican area. In January 1972, what began as a peaceful march against internment resulted in a massacre in the Bogside in which British soldiers opened fire on the unarmed protesters, killing 26 people. This day too would be known as Bloody Sunday. A cover-up ensued but it did not stop the huge anger from Catholics and a massive increase in recruitment to the IRA.

Protests in the H-Blocks

In 1976, Republican prisoners lost their 'political prisoner' status and were treated like common criminals, having to wear prison uniforms and losing other privileges. They refused to wear the uniforms and wore only blankets instead, demanding their 'political prisoner' status be returned. They organised the assassination of prison guards on the outside while their treatment in the prison became violently worse. The protests escalated into the Dirty Protests in which they refused to leave their cells, even for the toilet ... so it ended up smeared on the walls.

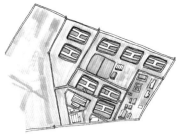

H-Blocks, the Maze Prison, Belfast

In 1980 seven prisoners went on hunger strike together, refusing to eat while demanding their privileges. After 53 days, one of the strikers, Sean McKenna, was on the brink of death when the government agreed to make changes. By the start of 1981, those changes still hadn't been made so even more prisoners went on hunger strike, one at a time to stagger the effects and increase their political strength. Bobby Sands was the first to go on hunger strike, and was the first to die. While he starved, he was elected as an MP. In total, ten hunger strikers died before British Prime Minister Margaret Thatcher gave in to their demands. All this allowed Republican party Sinn Féin to make a return in a new form.

1990s The Peace Process

CEASEFIRE

Violence continued in the North throughout the 1980s. The IRA kept up their bombing campaign in English cities too. Political pressure and public outcry at the atrocities grew and in 1994 there was a ceasefire called between the UVF, UDA and the IRA. Some wanted to keep fighting, some wanted to change. The year 1998 saw the Good Friday Agreement, which established that if a majority in the North and South wanted Northern Ireland to join the Republic, the British government would make it so.

Times have thankfully been much more peaceful in the North since. Strong political divides exist between Republicans and Unionists but at least they aren't blowing each other up! Power sharing occurs in the Northern Ireland Assembly in Stormont between Sinn Féin and the larger Democratic Unionist Party. The British Referendum to leave the EU in 2016 has raised a lot of questions in Northern Ireland. As of 2016, it remains to be seen what will happen regarding Northern Ireland and Brexit. Whatever the outcome, long may peace last!

SINN FÉIN

DUP
DEMOCRATIC UNIONIST PARTY

✗ YES

VOTE YES. IT'S THE WAY AHEAD.

END SECTARIAN MARCHES

RESIDENTS RIGHTS
ARE BEING TRAMPLED ON

A5

1990s-2000s The Celtic Tiger

Meanwhile in 1973 the Republic joined the European Economic Community which would become the European Union (EU). Being a mainly agricultural country, Ireland had struggled to get into the international market, relying on the UK for most of its trade. Most of Ireland's industry was built on foreign companies. The EU gave Ireland access to a bigger market and gain funding to improve Ireland's infrastructure. Emigration was still a problem in the 1980s but the 1990s saw the dawn of a new era in Ireland: The Celtic Tiger.

THE EUROPEAN COMMUNITIES

The 1990s brought a new confidence to Ireland. The Irish soccer team did well in the Italia '90 World Cup, which put everyone in a good mood! Things were more peaceful in the North and the world was loving Irish culture through shows like Riverdance. Irish people were able to stand tall and the economy reflected that too. As computers began to revolutionise the world, Ireland became a base for technology companies. Ireland's educated, English-speaking workforce offered skills and expertise in a growing and changing world.

HEY! COME DO COMPUTER STUFFS IN IRELAND! WE'S GOTS AN EDUMACATED WORKFORCE NOW!!

Ireland entered the 21st century and the new millennium with all the confidence in the world!

2008-2010 Boom to Bust

The construction sector thrived in the 2000s. Lots of houses were built and many people made lots of money buying and selling property. The European Central Bank (ECB) loaned a lot of money to Irish banks, further fuelling the economy but the bubble was ready to burst!

I DON'T KNOW WHAT A TRACKER MORTGAGE IS!

Banks across the world had given huge loans to people, who, in the long run, couldn't repay them. American banks had been selling these bad debts to each other, too. Eventually, in 2008, one bank was left holding all these bad debts (Lehman Brothers) and it collapsed, spreading panic to banks around the world. Banks were afraid to lend money in case they couldn't get it back. With their flow of money suddenly cut off, many building contractors here went bankrupt and left houses unfinished. People who'd bought during the boom now had huge mortgages on houses that weren't worth nearly as much any more.

WE'RE GONNA BAIL OUT THE BANKS!

Irish banks were in trouble and the ECB worried that they wouldn't get their money back, throwing Europe's economy into meltdown. They pressured the Irish government into bailing out the banks. Billions of euro of taxpayers' money was poured into the banks, one of which, Anglo-Irish Bank, collapsed anyway! A year later Ireland's economy was doing no better so the International Monetary Fund was called in to bail us out! It was a bit of a mess.

UM... CAN YOU BAIL US OUT PLEASE?

INTERNATIONAL MONETARY FUND

2016 - Ireland today

A few years on, harsh cuts in government spending and increased taxes have made life tough for a lot of people. A recovery is happening, but some people aren't feeling it. Increased rents, especially around Dublin, are creating more homeless, despite the many empty houses built around the country.

Times may be tough but positive things are happening in Ireland. Relations with the UK have improved. In 2013, Queen Elizabeth II became the first British monarch to visit the Republic. In 2014, Irish President Michael D. Higgins made a state visit to the UK. They were symbolic visits of peace, reconciliation and looking to the future as friendly neighbours.

I LIKE WHAT YOU'VE DONE WITH THE PLACE!

MARRIAGE EQUALITY REFERENDUM

YES

YAS!!!

In 2015, the people of Ireland voted to legalise Same Sex Marriage, showing a change in attitudes here and a willingness to create a positive future!

Ireland remains a strong figure on the world's stage in the arts. Successful writers, musicians, actors and directors present Ireland as an island of craic and culture. For a seemingly insignificant island on the very west of Europe, Ireland has had a huge influence on the world, culturally and historically. It is important to know where we have come from so we can have a better idea of where we might go! As long as we have each other, what's another year?!

Taoisigh of Ireland

The Taoiseach is the head of the Irish government and usually the leader of the majority party.

W. T. Cosgrave
President of Executive Council
(1922–1932)
Cumann na nGaedheal

Éamon de Valera
President of Executive Council
(1932–1937)
Taoiseach (1937–1948) (1951–1954)
(1957–1959)
Fianna Fáil

John A. Costello
Taoiseach (1948–1951) (1954–1957)
Fine Gael

Séan Lemass
Taoiseach (1959–1966)
Fianna Fáil

Jack Lynch
Taoiseach (1966–1973) (1977–1979)
Fianna Fáil

Liam Cosgrave
Taoiseach (1973–1977)
Fine Gael

Charles Haughey
Taoiseach (1979–1981) (1982)
(1987–1992)
Fianna Fáil

Garret FitzGerald
Taoiseach (1981–1982) (1982–1987)
Fine Gael

Albert Reynolds
Taoiseach (1992–1994)
Fianna Fáil

John Bruton
Taoiseach (1994–1997)
Fine Gael

Bertie Ahern
Taoiseach (1997–2008)
Fianna Fáil

Brian Cowen
Taoiseach (2008–2011)
Fianna Fáil

Enda Kenny
Taoiseach (2011– present,
as of 2016)
Fine Gael

Presidents of Ireland

The President of Ireland is the head of state, a ceremonial position elected by the people of Ireland. The President's term is seven years with a maximum of two terms. The President is responsible for signing bills into law, convening and dissolving the Dáil and represents the state in foreign affairs. S/he is also the supreme commander of the Defence Forces.

A presidential candidate can be nominated by at least 20 members of the Oireachtas, at least four county or city councils, or they can nominate themselves if they have already served a term. Usually a candidate would be backed by a political party.

Douglas Hyde
President (1937–1945)
All-party nomination

Séan T. O'Kelly
President (1945–1959)
First-term nomination: Fianna Fáil
Second-term nomination: himself

Éamon de Valera
President (1959–1973)
Fianna Fáil

Erskine Childers
President (1973–1974)
Fianna Fáil

Cearbhall Ó Dálaigh
President (1974–1976)
All-party nomination

Patrick Hillery
President (1976–1990)
Fianna Fáil

Mary Robinson
President (1990–1997)
Labour Party, Workers' Party
and Independents

Mary McAleese
President (1997–2011)
First-term nomination:
Fianna Fáil
Second-term nomination: herself

Michael D. Higgins
President (2011– present,
as of 2016)
Labour Party

First published in 2016 by
The Collins Press
West Link Park
Doughcloyne
Wilton
Cork
T12 N5EF
Ireland

© John D. Ruddy 2016

John D. Ruddy has asserted his moral right to be identified as the author of this work in accordance with the Irish Copyright and Related Rights Act 2000.

All rights reserved.
The material in this publication is protected by copyright law. Except as may be permitted by law, no part of the material may be reproduced (including by storage in a retrieval system) or transmitted in any form or by any means, adapted, rented or lent without the written permission of the copyright owners. Applications for permissions should be addressed to the publisher.

A CIP record for this book is available from the British Library.

Hardback ISBN: 978-1-84889-295-8

Design and typesetting by studio10design.ie
Typeset in Nothing You Could Say
Printed in Poland by Białostockie Zakłady Graficzne SA

Cover illustrations by John D. Ruddy